The Tie that Binds

*For Holly —
A token for a debt
that I may owe the
rest of my life.
Jon*

The Tie that Binds

The Poems of The Poet Preacher

Richard Carleton
Edited by Jon Carleton

iUniverse, Inc.
New York Lincoln Shanghai

The Tie that Binds
The Poems of The Poet Preacher

All Rights Reserved © 2004 by Jon R. Carleton

No part of this book may be reproduced or transmitted in any form or by any means, graphic, electronic, or mechanical, including photocopying, recording, taping, or by any information storage retrieval system, without the written permission of the publisher.

iUniverse, Inc.

For information address:
iUniverse, Inc.
2021 Pine Lake Road, Suite 100
Lincoln, NE 68512
www.iuniverse.com

ISBN: 0-595-32453-3

Printed in the United States of America

To Jane and Peter
Sister and Brother

The Tie That Binds

I'll be damned if I can remember
From September to September
Whether March 15th is Mother's Day
Or whether the 12th of that month is for
Mother and all others should stay away.

On one of those dates my father was born.
But both my father and my mother greet the "morn"
With such evident joy and youth
That I don't know their ages any better than
Their birthdays and that's the truth.

So I enclose these little verses
Hoping you both may have heard worse
And if there is now any doubt in your minds
That I think a lot of you, then you don't
Believe in the tie that binds.

Richard Carleton

Contents

Introduction xiii

Ties to Youth and Love 1
The Craftsman 2
Thoughts 3
Ambition 4
Philosophy 5
Frustration 6
Moment of Beauty 7
Atlantic Categories 8
Reaching for the Moon 9
Thoughts of Youth 10
To "Bright Morning" (Edith) 11
Dorothea 12
Harriette 13
A New Friend Becomes an Old One (Muriel) 14
Incident 15
Please Don't Talk About Me... 16
This Hour 17
On Reading My Letters to Others 18

Ties to Family and Home 19
To My Wife *20*
Home *21*
I Tiptoe After My Wife *22*
Why Didn't They Tell Us *23*
Twin-Bed Marriage *24*
After the Baby is Quiet *25*
I Want To Talk Children *27*
It Was While Kneeling *29*
And So To Bed *30*
To Marcia *31*
Message to the Chinese Communist *32*
Baby Girls *33*
Sunlight On My Son *34*
Pillow Play *35*
On Giving Thanks *36*
Like a Child *37*
Sniffer *39*
My Address *40*
Framework for Freedom *41*

Ties to Parents and Heritage 42
For February Fourteenth *43*
Mother's Day 1946 . . . . *44*
To Mother (1946) *45*
To Father (1946) *45*
Trauma *46*
To My Mother and Father *47*

Contents

Size 9, Brown	48
To Remember You	49
Heritage	51
Heritage II	53
For Christmas 1974	55
How We Fail	56
The Minister Looks at His Congregation	57

Ties to God and Nature 58

Religious Weather	59
Safe Days	60
Praise	61
Sun and Mist	62
Meditation on Noise	64
Listen	65
Quiet	67
One Day in October	69
Elements of Nature	70
I Sing	71
A Spot on the Window	73
Inside Out	74
For Every Day	76
Gifts Thou Hast Given	77
On Knowing	79
Out of the Bits and Pieces	80
Stream of Life	81
Sometimes—Not "Religiously"	82
Contrast	83

The Ecumenical Meeting *84*
Ready for God? *87*

Ties to Time and Myself **88**
On An Old Christmas Card *89*
I Remember—and I'm Thankful *90*
Income Tax Time *91*
Needs of People *93*
On Accepting People as They Are *94*
Who Sits With You? *96*
One Year Out *98*
Cold Hands I Loved… *99*
Inside of Me *100*
Popular Song *101*
The Old Clock Ticks! *102*
Who, Me? *104*

Introduction
Richard Carleton: The Man and the Poet

The character, as well as the career, of my father Richard Carleton may belie some misconceptions of a minister and poet. He has been no less the ordinary man for being an extraordinary creator.

What we learn is that the creator, the minister, the extraordinary man was merely the ordinary man intensified: a person whose life was sometimes lifted to a high pitch of feeling and who had the gift of making others share his excitement. The ordinary man Richard Carleton lived by the creative spirit. He thought in images of the family and dreams in fantasy like a child; he lived by poetry. I know this well because I am his son.

Yet he harbored a feeling of timidity in this endeavor. In his youth he had worried about not being able to express himself and he feared that he would not be understood. This book reveals his personal courage and conviction.

The extraordinary realization is that Richard Carleton was a thinker, poet, and scholar in the tradition of Emerson and Thoreau. It is my opinion that he was a Transcendentalist in the 20th century who gave private expression to his beliefs about—man, nature, and God—in his poetry and who later, took this art form to a higher level as public expression—to parishioners in his church prayers and prose. By breaking the shackles of his Victorian upbringing, Richard Carleton freed his own soul to say what he thought secretly in his heart openly from the pulpit. He rebelled against the dangers of economic materialism and orthodox Christianity of the Industrial Age. And in this struggle, he wanted to share an intuitive, experiential, passionate, more-than-just rational perspective of Christianity with the people in his church. He was talking about "new wine."

The Tie that Binds

We live now in the Information Age. We communicate by telephone and email or not at all. We are a knowledge society. Yet the moral task we face to free our souls remains the same as my father's time when it comes to hard living and honest thinking, never mind connecting in a relationship. You know exactly what I am talking about. And it is my guess that my father's poetry creates for us new possibilities; he opens up an old closet door, reveals some very special family secrets, and tells us we must break away from our personal complacency and also, that we cannot be seduced by the Philistinism of our present obsessions. Richard Carleton suggests, as Emerson did with "soft determinism," you may rebel against your elders in order to see your true self. Yes, you find your own home.

Any account of Richard Carleton begins with the times and places in which he lived. Descended from a long line of New Englanders rooted in the region since the Pilgrims landed, he was born in 1912 in Worcester, Massachusetts. His ancestry is English-Irish-Scottish. His mother was a proper child of the Victorian time; his father was a self-reliant success in the fast growing insurance business. Richard's early childhood memories are centered on 12 Clifton Street in Worcester, and later, through high school and college years, at 19 Grafton Street in Shrewsbury, and occasional visits to the paternal grandparents on 20 High Street in Plymouth. His mother, his father, his brother Tom (two years older), and Richard (and always, the favorite dog!). This Shrewsbury home we remember well and we often recall times at the summer place in Brimfield, Chebeague Island, and several more places that contain my father's memories of the family and his ties with each of us.

My father was in high school from 1927 to 1930, graduating second in his class. In the summers of 1929 to 1933, he played xylophone and drums and played in a dance band. He entered Harvard College and studied history and literature. He played in a band named "The Scarlet Troubadours" through college and on one particular summer, he went to church one Sunday "just for the hell of it." He stayed there with the minister and from that time on, thought of entering the clergy. That fall, his college roommate was too busy to take Marcia Smart, and the girl he had been dating for three years, to a big dance. The girl so pleased him that he later married her.

Having gotten the call, my father attended Harvard University Divinity School from 1934 to 1935, and then Andover-Newton Theological Seminary from 1935 to 1937. During those latter years, he lived in Boston and worked in halfway

Introduction

houses. He was ordained in 1937, and the first parish (1938 to 1941) was in Croyden, New Hampshire, and during the war years of 1941 to 1944, he preached in Westford, Massachusetts, and left the ministry for a short time to do defense work. He then moved back to New Hampshire in Pittsfield (1944 to 1948); Springfield (1944 to 1948) and East Walpole (1954 to 1962) in Massachusetts. From 1962 to 1977, he left the New England area (the "factory-towns and provincialism") and moved to Ripon, Wisconsin, where his reputation grew and skills as a poet-pastor flowered. He taught religion for Ripon College, acted in plays, and spoke fervently to a new community of friends in the Midwest. He and Marcia bought a brand new house, a big change from the parsonages handed to us. My father chose to retire in 1978 and after the death of his father, my mother and Richard returned to his boyhood home at 19 Grafton Street. My father suffered from Parkinson's disease and in 1988, he died, but not before telling us "to keep on learning for him."

The poems in this collection were written throughout his life experiences in the places where he lived and worked. His poetry was clearly written by faith. In several poems, my father gives an explanation of what home has always meant: for home is the center of life—no mere residence of the body but the axis of the heart; the place where affections develop themselves, where children love and learn, where two toil together to make life a blessing. The touchstone of his core belief came together in the poem, "Like a Child," and remains as a legacy to all of the family. It is a true prayer and wish to know that life is play.

At the same time, you will also picture in words the depths of want of my father; he says as a man that he was at times lonely and separate from those he dearly loved. True, life is a difficult journey, and like him, we are all on a pilgrimage. But when the distance had lost its enchantment and ardor for adventure had cooled, when fears had been bravely faced and wonder satiated, his heart longed for a resting place and this testimony was found in the poignant words of a poem, "Sometimes—Not 'Religiously'," that hallowed life and gave refuge to his creativity and soul.

Yet poor indeed is the person whose mind is not enriched by some phrase or moment of lasting truth and beauty that serves to restore the soul in the exigencies of life. I share one memory of me with my dad as we traveled in the car and no radio was to be played for my entertainment. So sitting beside him in that '54 Chevrolet, I asked him to sing, "Stardust," a number he used to do in the dance band. With both whistle and voice mastering the melody, he showed his stuff and the rhythm of the road followed in perfect harmony, and he mesmerized me with a moment I will always cherish. Oh, that was special! Each of us in the Carleton family has memories of a lovely time or poetic line to renew fellowship with each other.

In his poetry, you will encounter his questions and musings about life as a boy, his first love (Edith), the college girls (Muriel, Dorothea, and Harriette), his true love (Marcia), and private reflections about his parents, children (Jane, Peter, and Jon), the grandchildren, and a dog named Dierdre. Connections abound. The humor and seriousness has the power to surprise. As best I could, I arranged them so. And certainly, almost as great as his ability to write a line of personal truth is his ability to lift that line to higher levels of emotion and achievement.

To discover afresh his truth expressed with elemental force, our eternal kinship with one's father is a universal urge. "The Tie That Binds" had its origin in the recognition of this impulse. Here is the journey of the ordinary man we knew as my father; here are the extraordinary words of wisdom and thought of comfort for all of us. Consolation is the objective of "The Tie That Binds": to provide a key to the things of the spirit as inspiration for our daily living, its design, and its true purpose. I can only invite you to read.

Jon Carleton

Ties to Youth and Love

The Craftsman

A searing, white-hot flame,
Dirty brown ore,
The nerveless touch of the skilled workman,
And the work of art appeared...
Gold-glinting red in the firelight,
Strong, sinewy, exquisite...
How man's thought can flow through his fingers!

Ties to Youth and Love

Thoughts

Rocks, cliffs, masses of stone,
Golden, blue, and jagged.
Up—to the highest—and far below
A tint of blue.

Life is a climb
(to the top?)
Where, before all,
We can see the universe
Toiling and laughing
In blood.

Ambition

Lone Wolf, brooding o'er that cliff,
What do you mean by slinking?
Are you a warning?

Sleek, fine, gorgeous, gray wolf...
Why sit so crouching, ears cocked, body forward, silhouetted?
Watching the ribbon road below you.

How long have you sat there? Long? Is it long?

Will you be there always...
Watching—waiting—brooding—
Still so beautiful in the symmetry of that supple gray outline—
Bushy tail—healthy eye—teeth so white and strong?

Bent o'er the cliff—
Waiting—watching!

Where no one will ever reach you on that peak!

Ties to Youth and Love

Philosophy

With animals I've learned to know that death
And life and search of unseen thing is breath
Of all our being, doing, loving, hating:
Mercy tells me how God makes this mating!

Frustration

Out of the loneliness within my soul
I come to whom? Well, here and there
I've found a faith in friends, but not just where,
In love, the ordinary man is whole…
I say 'not love', for I have played my role
And found it wanting in full trust and care.
Something in me demands a loving rare
But does not give…but does not give "my goal?"

My solitude is tempered not by Him;
The you of you—the me of me—and what
Is this but sparks of light, now bright, now dim?
Some thing there is which I must find in time,
Some truth to try when I am aware of naught
But living life and loving! Truth in Time?

Ties to Youth and Love

Moment of Beauty

Do you remember now the hill
Where first you knew the simple life
Of good and ill?

October day with woods of green,
And yellow, orange, brown, bright red
Of autumn sheen?

The light, mist-rain as though a cloud
Had come to earth from worlds of words
Not said aloud?

The wind that whipped its bridal veil
In silver lines that streamed across
The open vale?

And how the sun shone through the rain
And rainbow wrote the day would come
Again—in pain?

Atlantic Categories

A bathing suit is scarcely chic at tea;
Tuxedos were not meant for jungle use.
And thus, today, we look at life—the deuce
Of spades should not be wild—it's parody
Of all that's really true! The tidy D.A.R.
(My dear!) would not be on the loose
If they should wish to ride upon a goose
Or wear a bathing suit. It should not be!

And if I write a sonnet praising love,
Would I then be a poet? The gentle dove
Lives ever and anon a well-bred life
Of dove-like softness and gentility,
And apes not apes. The witless human strife
For style creates peculiar comedy.

Ties to Youth and Love

Reaching for the Moon

The night was like a baked potato, black,
And Moon, our ship, was just a little wart.
The skipper had been drunk and lost his chart
And in the mottled, billowy sky, his knack
Of sailing gone, he nearly lost the track.
Across the Milky Way the flashing dart
Of a falling star brought cheer to the captain's heart.
He wiped his brow and peeped out through a crack:

A rustic bridge, a girl and I, upon a shelf
A land of light and shadow played upon by Pan.
The girl looked towards the moon and took my hand,
But I looked in her eyes and saw—a new self!
Just then the skipper stopped his ship of schemes
And threw those two the golden dust of dreams.

The Tie that Binds

Thoughts of Youth

A wind vane of ships I have!
For days they sail in peace.
Blithe, and Bonny, and Gay are they—
West Wind wafts.

For once they are mad!
Wet, and Cold, and Rainy day—
East Wind whines.

And I've no word from my love!

Ties to Youth and Love

To "Bright Morning" (Edith)

Pal, of the sweetest blue eyes,
I cannot but love you.
When I find a heart—so simple
It is great—of faith;
I am lost to find words
To open my heart to her,
Of the dearest love I have ever had.

The Tie that Binds

Dorothea

I drink to dream of the dark-eyed Dorothea!
In whom, though long I have not known the girl,
Have I met much to worship midst the whirl!
Did I say "Nuts"? Fool! Eyes in which the fear
Of watch-face in the dark showed stark the mere
Face of the child but in which does unfurl
At times a fine-spun force: Beneath the curl
Of modish hat is strength that faith finds dear.

I loved her as a summer love, and more—
For always when I searched 'dark eyes,' the lore
Of love lay lost, and seared deep in the soul,
Drank down the dregs of poignancy. To sate
This haunting sweetness I have found a goal:
For girls like her have made mere men stand straight!

Ties to Youth and Love

Harriette

The thought of you in "morning" red—a dark
Warm hue reflected in your dark-brown eyes
And tree-brown hair and grass-brown skin—the mark
Of one wild rose that in a lone spot lies:
The dark red of my Harriette, whose arms
Have held me close to prove the dance of life
A harmony of hues and lines, which calms
The fear that I alone must face the strife:
Behind those dark eyes surely there is power,
The greater when the years have proved this hour
Eternity of joy knit into one:
The heart that loves and gives—and eyes that wink!
The growing thought, Dear Girl of leaf-green Ink,
Of you and I as one, when life is done.

A New Friend Becomes an Old One (Muriel)

Asleep, I awoke to see you once again:
I thought how long I'd known you—how you'd grown
Within me since last summer—all the men
And women I have met and you alone
Stand well above the rest for something fine
Of cheerful courage to yourself and all.
For something clear and bright that's not quite mine,
In you I can't resist its quiet call.

She yet shall fail me, I have said, and more
That was not true to you or me, for I
Had hoped to find (what I know now) the door
Of an old and loyal friend, the quiet trust
That merely asks and gives and cannot die:
Like night and rain and fog and wind and dust.

Incident

The way of grief is not apart from life.
A smile may seem a momentary thing
Concealing friend and foe alike, but bring
To me a man whose mercy measures strife
Of heart and hand the same. The stainless knife
Of sorrow cuts at first the skin—the sting
Is light—but wider grows the bloody ring
Until with hopelessness the heart is rife.

I say give me the man whose song is strong,
For love has beauty though the man is wrong.

"Perhaps I should not tell. Your sweetheart bought
A ring today. I'm sorry, pal. And so—."

"I'd rather hear this news from you,"—I caught
His outstretched hand—"than any man I know."

Please Don't Talk About Me...

I'm the one to tell my friends,
Not you.
If I write, I write what I write
To you!
Let the artistry be mine
To give.
Friends to me but not through you.
Let live.
I don't want the judgment of friend through friend,
So smart…
The gossip, so sure, mind all made up…
No heart!
If I turn against you, I turn on myself,
How true!
But truth is to feel, to be what I am
With you!
Is love the reason for all your talk?
Or pride?
Whichever it is, it will shine out
From inside.

This Hour

This hour I cannot give you all I know—
That's why I wonder if my love is real.
The calm of thought at night now makes me feel
That somehow two may differ here below,
That somewhere here on earth I'll find a foe
Whose whip will wound my heart and raise a weal
Of flesh as token of a life-long seal.
But you alone can wash away my woe.

My love, you sew my wound but make the scar—
What kind of creature crucifies the flesh?
Hope within hope, my love, you cannot mar
My soul except through love caught mesh by mesh.
But if we are not one, I tell you now
That unto you this hour love brings a vow.

The Tie that Binds

On Reading My Letters to Others

Please don't share me with others, my love,
I want to be yours alone.

Let what I do, what I was, be a secret between us,
Let it be just what we are.

Let the others guess, outsiders they—
Let them gossip and wonder, admire.

Then if they know, they'll be part of us!
Friendship is thus—not words.

Then if we do not speak, but we will, we will.
We'll share true thoughts and deeds.

We'll be what we are, not once nor then,
Eternal with God, we are!

Ties to Family and Home

The Tie that Binds

To My Wife

Some nights I wish I were the husband of twins!
I love my wife, but—or and—how nice it would be
To have two of her, especially on cold nights,
With one on each side, all three of us curled up together.
I don't want a different girl:
I just want more of Marcia when she smiles,
When her eyes light up, when she's willing.
I never get enough looking and feeling to satisfy me.

What bewildering, delirious fun it would be
To see two of her undress!
And I love to see her walk from me
And I love to see her come towards me.
(Both the backs and fronts of knees are fascinating; and on
back or front are two round, firm, molded forms
with different ways of expressing themselves.)

Is it wrong to love my wife so?
No!

Home

I love the music my wife makes with the baby.
She talks. She hums snatches of songs.
She tells him he's big, he's older, he's doing new things.
Without knowing it, she moves quicker,
Acts faster than usual. Her eyes sparkle.
She bends over the crib and her body sways.

There's a line of harmony up the backs of her legs.
There's a sweetness to the shake of her hair.
Music? Music in person and voice and song and line:
Laughter and bubbles of sound.
The music of home and love.

The Tie that Binds

I Tiptoe After My Wife

I tiptoe after my wife to see our babies—
Is anything sweeter than sleeping children?
I watch them and get in the way
While their mother adds a blanket or shuts a window:
That little girl in the bed there is a part of me—
And the baby boy in the crib, what a feeling
Of kinship there can be between man and boy!
What have I done, O God? Or is it something
You are doing with me? Is there anything sweeter?
And more powerful than my own children
Sleeping in peace?

Ties to Family and Home

Why Didn't They Tell Us

Why didn't they tell us that children were such nuisances?
Before we were married—before we planned to have children—
Making us jump out of bed at midnight, or two o'clock, or
Four o'clock, or anytime we try to own a moment's rest;
And then wanting breakfast at five-thirty or six!
Fussing because they wish attention,
Or squalling because they get too much;
Taking our money, our time, everything we call our own—
Even ourselves; making us over in their image.
Born again? I'll say. I'll never be just me as I used to be.
Everyone told us about sweetness and such;
They all used words like 'cute' and 'cunning' and 'heavenly';
We even heard about sex.

But they never said anything about being obliged
To stay home with them every night, or about
How you have to teach them and teach them and teach them
(And reform your habits in the bargain), and how
You don't have time or energy for the violin
Or the dinner parties you were going to plan or
For 'leisure-time activity'!

No, it's—'Feed me, play with me, clean me, love me
Learn how to leave me, and then let me be myself!'
Who said anything about democracy? Babies are tyrants—
God's tyrants—enforcing the personal rule of love and care;
Enforcing it, I said, with no regard for us, or how tired we feel,
Or how much we want to do something else:
A personal rule, not a just one. Why didn't they tell us
God had such a terrible regard for the law of love?

The Tie that Binds

Twin-Bed Marriage

A woman should plan to go out every night
And a man to go out every day,
And so they can live all the rest of their lives
And never get in the way!

Ties to Family and Home

After the Baby is Quiet

After the baby is quiet, then there is time to love him.

At first you are too sleepy and cross, pulled out of bed
By his cries, and wishing someone else were up ahead of you.
The floor is cold and the stove is cold and the milk is colder still,
And the baby is cold and wet. So you change him and grimace
Mechanically, trying to make him smile. But he isn't fooled,
He's hungry. And now you're the one that's cold.

So you carry him by one arm and feel of the bottle—
But it's still cold, and you set it down again, the baby is mad,
And you walk and talk and sing and sit and get up again.
Why have babies anyway? But finally the time comes:
The time I am speaking of, I mean, when you rest
Your early morning bones in the maple rocker
And the baby grabs the bottle, and he's quiet.
Well, then there is time to love him.

Not that you stroke his head or cuddle him or bounce—
Let him drink, for heaven's sake.
But you love him in the best way, I think, for it is then that
You look around the room and think, after all,
You love your home and children.
You look down at his busy body, and sniff of his hair,
And one of his tiny hands (the little finger curls like Daddy's)
Reaches up and strokes your chin! Your little girl
Appears in the doorway, rubbing her eyes
And half in her bathrobe, immediately starts playing
With her doll where she left it the night before.

It's just a moment before the work of the day begins,
But it's a moment when,—well, maybe you think of God

The Tie that Binds

And wish you were pious enough to pray: For your heart
Is full of knowledge that you have a place in the world.
"The earth shall be full of knowledge of the Lord
As the waters cover the sea."
In your home, in your children.

After the baby is quiet, then there is time to love them.

Ties to Family and Home

I Want To Talk Children

I like the smell of a dog
And the feel of children climbing over me—
When I'm tired it eases my muscles to have them
Climb and slide off my back.

(Why? I don't know. My wife thinks I'm silly.)
And then it's fun to have the dog nose at my head,
Trying to find my face!
He thinks it's fun too.

This morning my son Peter struggled
Up into the Morris chair beside me,
Talking all the time the way he does,
Then he sat on his haunches at just my height and
Showed me two trains in one picture,
One right side up, the other upside down
(It's a remarkably interesting world.)

Sometimes when I say, "No, I'm tired,"
He crawls up behind me anyway.
How he doesn't lose his balance on the arm of the chair
On one foot I don't know, but I keep myself in
And trust in the institution God gave children
And he always makes it!
Then when I lie down on the couch
He clambers up the far end and snuggles down
In the crook of my arm. Which he does for half a minute—
And then I have to slide him off onto the floor, and
He laughs and begins again.

By this time my little black dog is jealous
And he sticks his wet nose up nudges my hand;

The Tie that Binds

Then Jane, my little girl, says, "Let's put Daddy to bed."
So I get covered up like a doll until it's time for dinner.

Do other parents like this, too?
I wish I knew.
I'd like to meet some parents who do.
I want to talk children and dogs and families and homes.

Ties to Family and Home

It Was While Kneeling

It was while kneeling on the granite floor
Doing defense-work (not praying, unless to work is to pray),
That I thought—
How empty life would be if I lost my little son!

That day in the harbor on his first motorboat ride
How he kept close to me, yet peered out over the edge
At the green water bubbled with white
While I took a strong grip on his jacket.
How the sun shone!

And the other people—peaceful, friendly,
My wife and daughter with us.
No, I'm not afraid he'll go to war (he's only two)
And I let him swing and climb his ladder and visit the neighbors
(I told him to give the neighbor's boy a "sock" if he hit him again,
To "look him in the eye.")
No, I'm just afraid of the emptiness life would be without him.
It is a thought, which keeps coming to me
In the midst of the war news—

I want to think about it a long, long time.

The Tie that Binds

And So To Bed

I was wishing they were both in bed, my two,
And Jane was a washbasin late.
Peter had gone ten minutes before,
There I was between "five" and "eight."

Was he ready to sleep, my five-year-old boy?
Well, one button was undone.
And Jane, where was Jane? Soap and water between—
Oh kids! Hurry up! Quit the fun!

I felt like a stomach-ache, scowling and cross,
I wanted to make something move—
The crank of the phonograph turned with my mood,
I balanced the point on the groove.

The call of the horns! The shriek of the flutes!
"The Skaters" are up and away!
Here's Jane! Seize her hand! Balance each, here we go—
Step, step—slide, step—step and away!

How sweetly she danced, my Jane, my Jane,
All in fun, before bed, age eight.
To the swing of the beat, round the hall, turn and skip—
Now three of us know how to skate!

So to bed, ends the day, and I chase them with slippers,
I open the window—a blast from the Dippers!
But I dream as I stride down the stairs with head high
How music and children keep happiness nigh.

Ties to Family and Home

To Marcia

I am strangely moved
When you sing beside me:
(Rare times when a minister gets to go to church with his wife).

We may not touch
But the sound of your voice
With me
Is a thrill I treasure.

Your voice has a lyrical
Innocent
Original
Sound of you.

No touch—no word—no look—
Just the sound
Of you with me.

The Tie that Binds

Message to the Chinese Communist

My Jon sits beside me and I love him.
Tonight he's quiet, content to sit,
Holding my book—no pictures,
Nothing of interest to his mind, except that
Daddy can read these little marks on paper.
"What's this number, Daddy?" "And this one?"
The radio talks the news—not good and we should listen—
But the real center of life is here in my big chair
With blond-haired Jon beside me,
One foot out the side, and one leg up by mine.

The man in Washington speaks to us.
That voice from Peiping—
Does someone there know how we sit,
And does he envy our freedom and love together?
Does he think we keep his food from him?
Or his right to speak?

Oh God, that's what we're trying to give him!
Will he take it—in any way—without hurting others
Because someone once hurt him?
Oh, the depth of the hurt of the world—
And how those who speak of war and hate
Show their own souls bare!
Four-year old Jon sits beside me—
And I am as God tonight.

Baby Girls

They ought to put tails on little girls,
To run and wiggle and wag;
And noses that wriggle, and sometimes curls;
And wrap them all up in a bag!

They might be provided with horns besides,
A devil in every dear;
And ears that would wiggle and lie on their sides,
To hear what they wanted to hear!

And wings on their feet but not on their backs;
They're pagan, if angels, you know.
But my little girl none of these lacks,
She's fitted from tip-ee to toe!

Sunlight On My Son

"Tell me a story, Daddy,"
My Peter said to me.
"Tell me a story with sunshine,
With hollyhocks and a bee."

Late winter's day was raw,
New snow bright on old,
And my little boy in bed
With more than a common cold.

"A sunshine story, Daddy,
With flowers yellow and bright!"
"Not black and brown," he told me.
(I looked out on the coming night.)

And we both dreamed of a garden
And spring in a little town
And a swing out near the sandbox.
('Don't make them black or brown!')

So we'd go forth together
With pitchfork and a rake,
A hop toad, a hoe, and a shovel,
And seed for the sun to wake.

Pillow Play

"P'lo! P'lo! P'lo!"
Said little Jane in her maple bed
Loving her papa's pillow—
"P'lo!" And she stood on her head!

She hugged it, she loved it, she squeezed it,
She tore the case in half.
She kissed it, she wet it, (she sneezed)
"P'lo!" And she laughed.

The Tie that Binds

On Giving Thanks

I am so thankful for babies like Jonathan
(He rolls his eyes to look at you—he smiles—
He tries to make up new words.)

I am so thankful for a wife like Marcia,
For Jane and Peter and Jon and all of them,
For Meagan and the angels round her bed—

My life is cells of thankfulness,
With a nucleus of the Holy Spirit
And cytoplasm of lives reaching out to each other—

Cells of thankfulness which make up my life: Everything!
Earth and grass and detriment of refuse,
Degradable, biodegradable: people!
Who are sons and daughters of mothers and fathers,
Grandchildren who will be fathers and mothers—

My gratitude is my attempt to love—
A list longer than life, longer than history,
As long as the creating Word of God!

I could sit here for ages and ages
Writing names and places, things and people,
All of my life I am
Drowning in it all.

It is all history,
It is all God, that is
God and me living forever, forever alive.

Ties to Family and Home

Like a Child

I want to be like a child—
I do not want to be a child.
I want to be a man who has the freshness of childhood,
The innocence to begin all over again,
The naiveté to make others begin over again with me.

To feel snow like a puppy, one paw in the air,
As out of the void of brownness
The world takes shape again.

To touch things, delicately, like fresh toys of childhood,
To know the precious things we longed for
As we went to sleep.

To have again all the time of life,
To carry an enormous load of responsibility at one moment
And then go home where someone else will take the load.

To be seen and not heard, like the old-fashioned child,
And, in the forced quietness, to discern
The disagreeableness of those who lay down laws,
The yearning of an aunt who never grew up,
The playfulness of a grandpa who knows that life is play.
To feel the shock of what death means to an adult,
Not the grief of the death
But the grief of the persons who feel the death.

To know all these things and pray in secret
That all the family will have their hearts' desires,
And that someday I will meet another child

The Tie that Binds

Who will feel as I do
And the two of us will face the world together.

To wonder how there can be so many different people
That heaven cannot hold them.
So many that only a God-beyond-imagining
Could look after them all,
And to leave it to Him.

Ties to Family and Home

Sniffer

I don't smell very good
But my dog does.
She sniffs.
In the house she just lies there
(unless anyone comes in)
And then she approaches with her nose,
Gets a whiff, and that's you.
Her real life is outdoors,
A walk with me, (the meaning of life to a dog
is to be out with the one she belongs to)
And at the same time she can roam and sniff.
The message is in the smelling.
Each has odor.
Some stink.
But Deirdre smells.
Well, that's life.

My Address

Now I am alone at night.
This noisy small town is still, and there is the comforting
Patter of rain on the tin roof near my window.
How I wonder about small towns and how small are they
And are the people here because they are old
Or did the town make them so?
The small town with its gossip and bickering
And its refusal to do anything if someone else will do it.
The small town and its interesting people
Who find time to live together
(If you stay long enough to notice it)
To have fun and do what they want to do, together.
The people who pause to think, who will not be rushed
Or commanded by the world.
A few people who think deeply.
And the many small children, acting tough, but really
Quite naïve about the affairs of the world.
Too naïve?
One of America's small towns,
One of New England's small towns,
One small town in New Hampshire,
Pittsfield.

Ties to Family and Home

Framework for Freedom

A framework for freedom is the countryside you love—
Where you were born and your fathers before you.

A framework for freedom is the opportunity to have
A place to stand: a piece of land, a job to do,
A service done for someone else—

A framework for freedom is a family—
Each a part of the family, creating a new family,
Seeing the creation of many new families—

A framework for freedom is the right to speak and write
And live without fear.

And that means that the government defends me
In my freedom (not the other way around).

The government defends me.
Else it has no being!

Ties to Parents and Heritage

Ties to Parents and Heritage

For February Fourteenth

I remember once when I kissed my mother,
She, in bed, reaching up her arms,
Smiled sweetly, and said:
"My, but your breath is sweet,
Richard!"

And when I came home from college,
She would kiss me and say:
"I hate to see you go—
When you are here I feel all smiles!"

Now I am away from home
And I wonder
Why the name Richard
Sounds so bold to me!

Mother's Day 1946

'Though there are times when parent and child
Have no speech or language,
'Though love always gives more than it receives,
'Though our place in life must be filled because
Our place in life must be filled (and for no other reason!)
It is better, so.

Better to *yearn* for understanding,
Better to *wonder* how love can be full,
Better to *keep on* trying to thank Mother—

For our understanding must be infinite,
Our love an eternal thing,
And our thanks never finished.

To Mother (1946)

This birthday card is the one you earned
Many years ago.
How sweet the tribute, only sought
By love's ebb and flow.

To Father (1946)

The many times I think of thee
Are strange delight and keen.
Discovered late, known silently.
Let's share, but not be seen!

Trauma

I made a special trip to have supper with my folks.
When I told Dad we were planning to leave old New England
To go off to the Midwest, he barely blinked—
But I knew his heart blinked too.

Later I had to write to them that
My home was really with my wife
And children, not with them—
My mother never could hear that kind of message.

A dear friend told me that she and her husband
Might be confirmed in the Episcopal Church.
It's one thing to be an Episcopalian in a Congregational Church—
That's one of the things the Congregational Church stands for—
But it's quite another thing to be deliberately different,
To belong to a different people!

I wonder if I showed my sinking heart?
When the Mass was changed from Latin to lingo,
Someone had been thinking who did not feel.
People feel—for a reason!
Take away the chance to feel
And you have taken away the reason.

Oh, my sinking heart—Does my friend know?
How can—and I stop—mid-thought.

Ties to Parents and Heritage

To My Mother and Father

You haven't discovered all about me yet—
Perhaps no one has, least of all myself.
But I have treasures yet to give
Far beyond the little I have been.
And giving is creating.

What wonder human beings disagree—and criticize?
And then speak praise too late.
How great the faith in talent still unborn—
How far the fall when such faith finds no answer.

To my friend I can say these words but most of all
To those who know me best.
For to know is to see more and ever more
And more beyond what you see.

To know best is to wonder; doubt, the most!
How odd the spirit—yet spirit will lead
Faith on far ahead. You haven't discovered all about me yet.
You say it too.

Size 9, Brown

I buried my mother in these shoes.
They weren't very good even then
Four years ago.
Now I use them as paint and garden shoes.
I look at them and remember those last days
With my mother.
I remember the year or two before
When she wanted me to stay
As her little boy.
She was an ideal mother.
She enjoyed it!
Like a nun loving her work
More than God.
I finally got away…
But now I look at the shoes
For soon I must throw them out.
They aren't very good shoes.

Ties to Parents and Heritage

To Remember You

Something moves me to remember you
    The words you spoke
    The messages you sent
    Your hand upon my arm
    What you said
        And what you did not say.

To remember your need for me
    And my need for you.
        That's what it really is.

Yes, there are problems—and hurts—
    And tragedies of our own making:
    How we chose our friends
        And how we said the harsh words.

Tragedies we try to cover up
    By eating too much
        Or drinking too much
            Or working long hours
                Or trying to make up too much.

To remember you
    And the foolish predicament
        Or being fooled by your own love.

To remember you
    And the brave moments—
        The tears there behind your eyes.

The Tie that Binds

To remember you
    And how you learned to love,
        How you learned to let the great love happen.

To remember you...

Heritage

"Caroline"
Name on a glass paperweight
Made like a book with lines and name engraved.

Old
One hundred years or more
Out of date and into date again like a popular song.

Mine
Passed to me by my vigorous eighty-year-old Dad
Caroline was his grandmother and my great grandmother.

Meaning
Meaning of generations
Because Dad had to live with his grandmother when he was a boy.

Thing
Little old thing, which is an ordinary paperweight
Ordinary meaning to you and quite extraordinary to me.

Personal
To see my Dad in the perspective of my middle age
To touch on how a life comes out of a family
And how much family meant once and to know it still goes on.

Time
Each baby is born into a new family
And every new person in a community joins a new church.

Glass
Glass to see through and yet to see into

The Tie that Binds

Glass so breakable yet so clear—like the lines of heritage
Handed on.

Caroline
Caroline Crooker of Bath, Maine
I never knew her but she is in me as all
Grandmothers and grandfathers are in great new sons.

Glass
Time Personal Thing Meaning Mine
Old Caroline—Caroline Crooker of Bath, Maine.

Ties to Parents and Heritage

Heritage II

Grandfather was not much of a "Grandpa" in the sentimental sense,
But he was kind to my mother.
He was a little apt to be kind to any good-looking girl.
And Mother was sweet enough.

All of this helped balance our visits there
For Grandma would tip the scale towards Dad
And Grandpa—when he was around!—sure tipped people
One way or another.

He had quite a voice with the timbre of the old-fashioned whisper
Heard in the highest gallery,
A moustache, and he wore an onyx ring.
The ring had a big "C" for Carleton in the middle of it.

The other half of this story is about Dad and Mother;
They had to marry early because of love.
Not the pseudo-love of today's sophisticates,
But the feeling that each had to have the presence of the other
In order to be a complete person. That's love.

Father gave Mother a ring with a tiny diamond
And they were married and lived happily ever after.
(This is a continued story…)
But Dad was successful in selling
(And still is)
And maybe I was twelve years old when he bought Mother
A better ring.

And Grandpa died, and Mother had his ring,
And she had the jeweler take out the "C"

The Tie that Binds

And put the tiny diamond in its place,
And she gave it to me.

And when I look at the big old ring with its white-silvery center
I think of all these people and their history and their love
And that's heritage, too.

Ties to Parents and Heritage

For Christmas 1974

I am holding a child in my arms—
I am holding a child in my arms—
I am holding a grandchild, my great grandchild.

I am holding a child I am teaching—
A child of my talent, my responsibility—

I am holding a child of my neighbor.
My neighbor of South Boston, Roxbury, Dorchester,
My neighbor of Saigon, of Rio de Janeiro,
Of the waters off Hong Kong.

I am holding a child.
The child is either me or Christ.

I have not lived all of my life yet,
When I have lived all of my life
Then I will know how the child is
Both me and the baby Christ.

Until then,
To pray is to work

And to work is to pray.

The Tie that Binds

How We Fail

We fail in the depths of life—
Women and men seeking new relationships
Get to thinking
Only of themselves
And they reckon not the need
For family.

A family to be with,
   To come home to,
      To hide with,
         To confide in,
           To deal with,
              To care for,
                 To run away from,
But mostly to be there.

We are not much
   Without family
      And modern man is mixing himself up about it.

The Minister Looks at His Congregation

I wish my father were here—
And my mother—
To hear my words this morning,
The thoughts that race
Then stumble
    Through my mind.

We used to have good talks together,
Or silent times
    We understood.

After dinner it was, with all sitting around before a song,
Or sometimes on a hill looking off.

I look now at the faces before me and I see my mother and father.
I have so much of their mind in mine.
Through them—from this point on—I learn the mind of Christ.

How strange to think they are not here,
That they are older now, or ever change, or leave—

I wish my father were here—
    And my mother.

Ties to God and Nature

Ties to God and Nature

Religious Weather

Cloud versus sun
On Sunday.

The pagans named the day,
Christians only wanted to be *first*.

First-day versus Sabbath:
Seventh, the rest after creation—
First, the creation beginning with resurrection—

A belief:
Cloud to some,
Sun to others.

God above!

Safe Days

Safe days are stormy days,
When the spirit rises to meet the wind
When the nerves harden themselves
Against coldness and wetness
When we are aware of danger
And aware of God.

Sunny days are easy,
Warm days are fun.
God has given me a day
In which I can be one.

That's the day to pause

You must share the day with God!

Ties to God and Nature

Praise

Oh God!
Oh Now!
Oh Lovely, Fresh, Cool, Stirring, Changing—
Color in all and color in small—

Far out and far in—
Eyes overwhelmed, nerves speaking directly to mind,
Wonder of the wideness of the world—

We walk in beauty,
And we say
Creation is good—
And we *rest*.

Sun and Mist

Gold sunshine shone on golden leaves,
Against the darker shade beneath,
The red and green, the brown branch sleeves.

Gold too were the fields, pale stubbly gold,
There, by the wall a splotch of scarlet,
Above, in the blue, white clouds rolled.

I loved it there and sat in the sun,
The autumn hillside a gift of God.
Still solitude inside is fun.

Then suddenly came across my sight
A mist of rain from cloud too near—
Too near the earth to stop its flight.

Before my eyes wind whipped the mist,
Blew it in lines of tracing lace,
Never saw I such beauty exist!

Parallel lines of translucent rain,
Like Euclid proving Einstein wrong,
Or Pegasus streaming a silvery mane!

Parallels crossed by rainbow hues—
Glory! Glory! Thank you, God!
Rainbow and autumn and silver transfuse.

This was a moment of more than beauty,
September day I sat in the sun—
Come back, O Soul, come back to duty.

Ties to God and Nature

Gold sunshine shines in memory,
Angels' silver on hill and tree,
Like first-love treasured secretly.

Meditation on Noise

There is a machine-like hum from the city:
- Cars and trucks
- Wind up an asphalt avenue
- Staccato of the open engine of the cycle
- Shriek high and low of police siren
- Roaring saw on a diseased elm
- Long cry of the factory whistle at five o'clock
- Groaning horn of the freight train
- Radio chatter and chitter
- Comments on the weather

There is what we call quiet in the country:
- Wind in the trees
- Rain on the roof
- Birds telling us it is dusk on a cloudy midday
- Birds rattling on the trunks of resonant trees
- Pheasants going "squalk-squalk"
- Thunder
    - Air in the ears
        - And a bell from a cow.

In the country something is always calling.
There is noise in my heart sometimes:
- The rush of nerves
- The pound of pulse
- The shout of feeling guilty
- The siren of being pushed to keep up
- The words I want to remember to put in a letter
- The hope that God will give me quiet.

Listen

Listen to the beating heart of the world:

The cry of loneliness—

> Loneliness of the child wondering about the future—
> (And whether these people are really his parents),
> Loneliness of the youth daring the world, trying—
> Loneliness of middle age, the yearning for personal recognition—
> Loneliness of old age (I remember so much!)
> Am I remembered and cared for?
> Loneliness of no loved one there—
> Loneliness in the city street—
> Loneliness of being different—
> Loneliness of sin, my own choice separating me from others!

Cries from the desert
> Cries from the flood
> Cries from the poor
> Cries from the selfish
> Cries from the gut
>> from the nerves
>> from the soul.

Listen to the thanks of people:
Songs of gratitude, appreciation of beauty

There is the song of innocence and love
There is the quietness of contentment and the silence of awe.

Listen to the shouts of people:
> Shouts to win!
> Shouts of anger!

The Tie that Binds

       Shouts of danger!
       Shouts at play!
       A shout from one mountain
To another "hallooooo" down the valley
We are all one together.

Listen to nothing:
Wait for the Word—

    There is the un-said
    There is what cannot be heard
    There is what cannot be believed except by the one

    Who knows he cannot tell the person who does not know,
    He need not tell the person who does know.

God, Thou art mine and no one's else!

Quiet

The nature of quiet is the quiet of nature—

I mean heartbeats,
    Birdcalls,
    Leaf rustles,
    Squirrel chatter,
    Train tone downwind distance,
    Children at their fight play.

I mean breathing,
    Mind pulse and body pulse,
    Letting the tense shoulders go,
    The guts,
    The toes.

I mean questions,
    Where am I in life?
    Whom do I owe my life to?
    Is there a person in the mind of the universe?
    Will an eternal life be born out of this one?
    What will be my judgment day?
    Will I taste and feel and know again?

The nature of quiet is the quiet of nature.
    A blue lake,
    A bird trill, trill, trill
    Waves of water lightly tapping the shore
    Doldrum fly
    Fish pops the pond
    Light whish of leaves

The Tie that Binds

Listen!
I feel peace inside.

Some day
> When industry has moved to the side of the road
> Where the race of men goes by
> A man may get into a muffled train and ride to the city
> Where he will step into quiet—

And the new city of man will show him the nature of God.

Ties to God and Nature

One Day in October

Beneath the brackish blue of newborn dawn
The end of summer was foretold by sign
Of changing leaves, while gloomy green of pine
Ground sharp the rising sun of autumn morn.
This day the silky lake looks pale and wan;
This day the season's parting song is mine;
The pro and con of life on which I dine.
My body breathes a dirge of season gone.

The dreary waste of soul in city life
Is seen in walls that make a neighbor new.
My strength is wasted by the noise and strife,
My mind has wandered far from what is true.
This day the withered rose still holds a thorn,
But in my memory nature's law is drawn.

The Tie that Binds

Elements of Nature

Why are the elements of nature such music to us?
>The hish and hush, the roar and shriek
>Of wind—
>The drip and drop, pit and pat, slurp and gurgle
>Of rain—

The far sounds
>Bounded by how they bounce off hills and homes:
>Oh, I mean train whistles,
>Men at soccer,
>An owl heard near—far—to the left—off in the wood,
>Or a cantor singing from a hill across the valley to me.

Fire crackles,
Cold cracks,
Heat makes loud into quiet—

Quiet gives birth:
>And flies and frogs and bees and birdcalls—
>The legs of katydids,
>A leaf falling—

>—

>Music!

I Sing

I sing to the universe and I sing to the blade of grass—
I sing to my love and I sing to the vacuum cleaner—
I sing with the birds, I hum with the bees—
I am the one with the bud and the blossom and the seed.

I am seed and I am food,
I need food and I give food,
I am eco-balanced with all elements of the world.

I am a song, I am a singer,
I am sound, I am the quiet of the "rest,"
I am the beat—beat—beat of the full melody,
The rhythm of on and off, on and off, on and off on and off.

So sing to all life,
Life in the dirt, life in the air,
Life by the volcano, life far underground,
Life out on another planet…

I sing. I sing to the spirit of life.
I have to sing *to someone.*
We sing together and separately
But our singing is our celebration that we are both of us singers;
We are all of us—songs—we are all singing—
Singing of what happened today and what happened yesterday
And what will happen tomorrow—
New songs and old songs,
Our song and someone else's song.

The Tie that Binds

I sing the song of people who have been part of me—
All the peculiar, pretty, halting, proper, loving, selfish, wonderful
People.

Out of this I make my own melody to sing
To sing to Thee, God!

Ties to God and Nature

A Spot on the Window

A bird flew against our window,
Shocked itself,
And dropped to the ground,
Dead.

There is a spot on the window where I washed it
Clean only a few days ago.
This was life, God, now stark and gone.
I cannot pray to Thee for favors.
My way of living killed his way of living.
I am part of this.
I sin.

What will be my future?
Will more life of the wilderness be lost forever?
And man's forms of life take its place?
What life does man draw to him?

God help us? For what we spawn are
Squirrels and ants and gulls and skunks
And rats and viruses.
What can we lose?

Inside Out

If I could be turned inside out, God,
Someone would see spots
of envy,
         jealousy,
                  prejudice—

Spots that don't show on the outside.

If I could be turned inside out,
I would have to be washed,
              scrubbed,
                    scraped,
                        patched.

Wash me thoroughly, God,
Purge me
       so that I shall be clean.

If I could be turned inside out,
I might not be recognized
For my "coat of many colors"
                would not cover me.

But my neighbor might be turned inside out, too,
And I would laugh and laugh and laugh
Until I saw that he was laughing at me
And then I might cry.

God, if You would turn me inside out,
I know You would make me new.

From the inside out, I would be a new person.
From the inside out, I would know who I really want to be.
From the inside out, I would have to begin with honesty,

Ties to God and Nature

Justness,
> Sympathy,
>> And a smile for others.

If I were turned inside out,
I would have to be real
> With You.

The Tie that Binds

For Every Day

O God of common men, in what or where
You are, come look on me and shame me not.
Sometimes I've thrown away what you have wrought
And bought my bit of dirt, but always care
And sorrow made me pay a double share.
In youth I learned what toys tricks have taught—
And if there's more in years, I know I ought
To thank the everlasting hills in prayer.

O God Eternal, give me breadth and height;
Let me forget the signs of "Stop" and "Go"
And overlook machines that crush man's might,
Which show him not within himself the foe.
O God of Hills, let all my strength laid bare
Find love beneath an advertisement's glare.

Ties to God and Nature

Gifts Thou Hast Given

God, I wish I did not have to be ashamed
Of the gifts Thou hast given,
But I am. I am ashamed of what
I have done with them.

Thou hast given us this earth,
Full of beauty and wonder and change
And all forms of life—
And we contaminate it with refuse and filth,
Signs and junk and concrete,
And outhouses for this and that,
And then we look at it all and say,
"Pop! That's art!"

Thou hast given us air to breathe—
Yet now where so many people live,
The air is cloud and smoke and stench
And gas and dust—and we breathe it
Into our lings and catch it in our eyes
And offer it to our children.

Thou hast given us water to drink—
And mostly we make it undrinkable.
We fill it full of awful offal
And the life in it dies
And the detergent bubbles rise
And what then shall a child have to drink,
Poor child?

Thou hast given us fire—
Fire to warm us when it is cold,
Fire to temper steel,

The Tie that Binds

Fire to give energy that can travel by wire
To run our machines,
Fire to hurt and kill with,
Fire in the nuclear bomb—

God, we play with this fire
Like a child with matches.
Is the framework for the universe fireproof?

Earth, Air, Water, Fire—
Aristotle called them the elements of life.

I wish I did not have to be ashamed…

Ties to God and Nature

On Knowing

What do I know that I don't know?
>The wonder of life in the seed
>With all the plan for that particular plant,
>The beauty of a curved line in space,
>The return of geese over miles and miles and miles,
>The odor of a wine made from rose leaves,
>A misty-eyed, silent farewell (the last goodbye…)
>The satisfaction of a drummer as he continues
>The best of the march after the band has played,
>The symbol of sounds which become letters
>And words and meaning between us,
>The taste of a cool drink on a hot day,
>Or a hot drink on a cold day.

What do I know that I don't know?
>The given-ness of life,
>Its infinite-smallness,
>Its infinite-greatness,
>It infinite on-going-ness,
>Infinite with-us,
>Infinite nothing, like a snowflake.

What do I know that I don't know?
>My words with the Word of God.

The Tie that Binds

Out of the Bits and Pieces

Out of the bits and pieces of my life
I come to God.
How else?

From the TV drama
From the letters I should write
From people who want things done
From job and money and piles of papers
From headache and sorrow and even the joyous laugh
Which can come with sunshine and friends.

I do not know how to be ready for God—
I just have to try.

I come to the glorious Source of all beauty and strength,
I come to the Subject of our lives and thought,
I come to the Person who makes us sing and wonder and cry,
I come to a new chance, a new day, a new moment, a new life.

This is my God.

I see the bits and pieces of an enormous jigsaw puzzle of life.
God puts the picture before me.

Stream of Life

O Answer in Silence
    Wonder in Life
        Point in Space!

All names are less...
All names presume, blaspheme!

"Thou has deceived us, and we are deceived."

We happened.
We are a happening
Live, struggle, laugh, plan, push, bite, kick, smile, walk, talk—

It all happens to us.

Shall we ask for more
To happen?

The Tie that Binds

Sometimes — Not "Religiously"

Sometimes in the quiet of the night
When I am alone or others are sleeping—

Sometimes when the rhythm of the rain on the roof
Shuts out the other noises—

Sometimes when the heavy fog comes, and the trees are odd
Shapes of darkness against white—

Sometimes when the music holds me so that
My body does not move but my mind lives in the sound—

Sometimes when I rise and do the right thing
As though the Holy Spirit were guiding me—

Sometimes when I look at my companion
And see beauty there—

Sometimes in the fascination of the sulfurous city,
In people's faces and how they walk and the sign and smells
And the intricate depths and fantastic heights—

Sometimes in the memory of a little white chapel
Or a centuries old cathedral
Or the little ugly church people love—

Sometimes, I say, when life makes me pause, I present myself
And my needs and the thanks and the importunity of the world
To Thee, God.

Sometimes.

Contrast

To add height
To where he stood in the colonial pulpit
My old minister
Stood on a board
Marked "A. J. Gifford."

A. J. was his biggest contributor.

In my pulpit
I have an old strip rug,
Strip-braided by my mother-in-law,
Which came from the old summerhouse
On the island off Maine
Where we now have a new cabin.

It quiets my feet.

You certainly could say
It's what I preach on.

The Ecumenical Meeting

I peeked in the door
and the Episcopalians were

telling stories and laughing
and congratulating each other.

Then they got serious
and clattered up front
clatter-clatter bang-bang
with low words all
mumbledy mumbledy.

They didn't hear or see anyone else.

The Congregationalists told how it had been
and how it was going to be,
Not many there.
Those there were supposed to tell the others.

Anyway
They thought and thought and thought
about it.

The Unitarian speaker
gave an address
on how religion should be
social action.

No one was there.
but a cassette
for later study.

Ties to God and Nature

The Roman Catholics used to believe
they had the truth in the mystery.
They didn't know what the mystery was
but they all believed they had it
and out of that came truth, beauty, love, light.

Everyone else
Believed after them,

until one day some leader
said there was nothing there
and all the people agreed
(like the child watching the Emperor's parade)
and as soon as they saw nothing
they saw nothing.

Now there are some Catholics who believe
the mystery is the mystery
and lots of others trying to be
protestant Roman Catholics.
They don't make'em like they used to.

The E and R people
gathered in the hall
and drank beer.

Like the husband and wife who quarreled
until the wife said, "I wish I were in heaven,"
and he replied, "I vish I vas in the beer garden."
"Yah!" she cried. "Always you take the best!"

They believe and they enjoy it.

I can't imagine how those Fundamentalists
Freaks—Fools for Christ

The Tie that Binds

how they
flood the market—and how they
say the same thing to each other
and say it's new
and the same
and say it'e new
and say…
They sing it,
They say it,
They swing and sway
like hey hey hey!
like the joy of our commercial
Christmas
Everywhere, everywhere
Blocking the light.

The Methodists hang around
Outside
Grinning and slapping each other on the back.
(They're sure of their jobs.)

The Jews are the only ones
who have never been converted

except for people in general.

All there is left

is God.

Ties to God and Nature

Ready for God?

God, when we are ready for Thee
    We are not proud
    We are not asleep
    We are not hurting someone else
    We do not hate someone else
    And we are not sorry for ourselves
    Nor are we sure we are right.

When we are ready for Thee
    We shall be hungry and crying; we shall be dying
    We shall be going along a road too weary to go on
    We shall be looking in blackness for light we have not yet seen
    We shall have given up trying and come to letting ourselves go
    We shall have been speaking a cheery word and singing
        like the boy who sang the music of the spheres
    We shall have given a coat because the wind is cold,
        or some bread because we knew what it was to go
        hungry, or a word of faith because we had lost ours
        and we did not know it was there again but when
        we opened our mouths, we gave—

Life is a moment of shadows
        On the snows of Thy unseen life
            And Thy breath is in the wind…

Ties to Time and Myself

On An Old Christmas Card

When I was a boy I yearned for a friend,
A friend who would touch me inside.
I treasured the thoughts that gave me a place
In a world so vast and wide.

But I went to my room and wrote in a book,
Wrote other man's thoughts, not mine.
Well, once I did, but mostly I felt
That someone should know my shrine.

"How fortunate at Christmas-tide
Are those who have a friend!"
I pasted the card in my best book,
The one I would never lend.

I remember also a line from a lad
When I didn't expect the thought:
He said in words what I tried to do—
I suppose, he too, forgot?

Or is he like me a-wondering now,
Alone by a Christmas fir,
Of the good times we had, what we did together,
And what makes a friend entire.

The Tie that Binds

I Remember — and I'm Thankful

When the little girl came to the door and said, "Want to buy…?"
I love little girls who are so bright and friendly—And I know they
Tremble inside with the quick smart remark
That almost is spoken.

When my wife doesn't make the first helping so big, so that
I can have a second one—

The time something told me to take those few steps with
Rev. Dr. Fletcher, whom we had just made Minister Emeritus.
He was old and halt and courageous, and I was young and foolish, But
    something made me walk with him.

When my Dad took the punishment for me—
(I had put my hands on the newly painted furniture in the factory,
But he said he had—I was less than thirteen).

The Sunday the Pastoral Committee called
And my suit was threadbare and as I talked with them,
My little son climbed up on me so naturally
And I knew all would be well.

Strange moment when I was leaving a parish and
It came clear to me that in spite of difficulties and shortcomings
On both sides that I was the pastor of a people, and
Suddenly that place would be void—never to be the same,
Only healed by time and a new pastor.

Letters I have received thanking me for words I never said—
The times I have been called and knew I could.

Income Tax Time

What have I given?
> A man came to the door and I gave him something for food

I waited for my wife and opened the door for her—
> And I waited again
> To find out what we could do together—

I could not sleep because
> I thought my son had his life-values all mixed up
> But in the morning I knew I was wrong
> And I trusted him again.

I gave two dollars to another man at the door
> (How do they know where the minister lives?)

And I supported the Community Chest
> And pledged to the Church
> And subscribed to the Building Fund at my school.

I took a little time to see my mother and dad—
> Not much, but that little was doubled
> Because of memories.

I did my best to help
> A family situation—in-laws (and outlaws!)
> I did my best to serve in my job—
> I wrote to Senators and Congressmen and state legislators

The Tie that Binds

I tried to see and help the Church—imperfect instrument
But a lot better than anything else put in its place.

I try to keep strong and healthy—

Can I get credit for these things?

Needs of People

The first need is how to adjust—

How-I-was-brought-up to how-you-were-brought-up:
Me to my mother and father,
Mother to her mother and father,
Father to his father and mother,
Each to the other—
To how each was brought up—to me.

Wife—to what society says is a wife,
Husband—to what society says is a husband,
And how each breaks away.

The second need is how to be one's own self—
The mystical versus the measurement,
Genes versus the Holy Spirit,
Being told 'I know who you are' and therefore,
Being someone different. I must be a secret self!

The third need is how to be free—
Never to be cared for (even by God!)
The elder-elder land is a never-never land.

I don't believe in being tired,
I don't accept weak eyes or legs,
I am I, whether eight or eighty.

These are my real needs.

On Accepting People as They Are

On accepting people as they are—
What an infinite problem!
I am I—you are you—
I meet you—you meet me.

We try to say "tolerance,"
We have "Robert's Rules of Order,'"
We believe in families and the blood tie,
We go to counselors.
We even echo the sandlot cry,
"What's fair for one's fair for the other!"

When what we are really thinking about
Is having our self accepted.
Then we might accept someone else!
When our ship comes in,
When our talent is acclaimed,
When recognized and justified all in place,
Then we will look at others.

Ah, it doesn't work that way—
We have to develop the self
At the same time that we are living.
With an opposite self, an opposite sex,
An opposite elder.

Ties to Time and Myself

Getting along with neighbors,
Taking orders from a boss,
Disagreeing over politics,
Arguing about religion.

Accept those people?
What a problem for the infinite!

The Tie that Binds

Who Sits With You?

Let's imagine a chair—

Put it here in the center of the room—

Like—the old Salem rocker, with someone who sits and knits.
    —the Duxbury chair, with someone who is writing a letter to you, perhaps.
    —the Windsor chair, waiting for someone to draw it up to the table so we can have dinner together.
    —the old kitchen chair where husband can sit and tell his wife the news.
    —the great (big fat tall) rocker which came down from grandma, but the three-year-old is sitting there copying his elders. (He holds the magazine upside down, makes noises as though reading, then laughs ha, ha, ha, ha, ha, ha, ha…)
    —the great porch rocker (Jack Kennedy) which is so comfortable, either to rock in or to let the worker rest with his feet up on the rail.
    —the bench out of the porch which is handy for picnics or for standing on or for putting down a burden.

Armchairs
    And chairs without arms
    And overstuffed chairs
    And the cane-bottomed chair
    And the stiff ladder-back
    And the modern ones you pile up in the air
    And the stools and loveseats
    And even just cushions on the floor.

Ties to Time and Myself

Chairs in a circle for games and talk

    Solitary chairs for sorrow
    Chairs to rest in, to read in, to snooze in

    Chairs for people who are happy
    Chairs for people who are sitting up from an illness
    Chairs for people who drop in and tell us the news

    Beanbag chairs for people to droop into

    People in these chairs

Haven't you been praying?

One Year Out

Retirement is not having to do what you had to.
I don't like it that way.
I want to retire to new requirements
(Really, the old requirements on a new plane).

Someone should say:
    "You must have a sermon by Sunday."
    "You must call at the hospital."
    "You must…someone is depending on you."

Now—
    My wife says I must have better manners.
    My doctor warns, "You must be moderate."
    My dog puts her paw on my knee and says,
        "You must take me for a walk!"

Doesn't anybody want me?
    My thought?
    My cheer?
    My faith?

Ties to Time and Myself

Cold Hands I Loved...

I'm getting used to cold hands
This winter

Whether I owe them to Nixon
Or the oil-coal-nuclear barons
Or just man's selfishness
I'm not sure.

As long as I can feel the cold
I know there must be warm blood in my heart.

But when my extremities
Touch someone else—
Ouch! Like a hot stove.

But it isn't,
It's my cold hands.

I feel like sitting
On my hands—
Do nothing
But burrow.

My hands touch
Fevered hot hands
In the hospital:
We both say
"How good it feels!"

What else can I do
This winter
With my cold hands?

Inside of Me

While I stand there,
Thinking what to say,
The other person
Thinks that I have not heard
Or understood—
But I
Am contained
Within myself
(Like Jack Benny, "I'm thinking! I'm thinking!")
But by then I begin
To come out of myself
So that I can respond with all
Of myself.
You see, it has to come
Out of where I keep myself.

Popular Song

In England
O who will rub my tomb when I'm gone?
Gruesome and cold,
Stone next to bone,
Knees not in worship,
Bursitis in cursed hip,
Long paper tracing of me on a wall!

In USA
O who will desecrate my grave when I'm gone?
Knock over my tombstone—
Chop off the old chip—
Plastic Christmas wreath in April—
Superhighway death and thrill:
Pleasant load of humus litter on me!

In My Dreams
Let my dog lick my face one more time—
Let the church be silent—
Hide me from the law—
And the relatives.
Quick, let some flowers grow
Out of me!

The Tie that Binds

The Old Clock Ticks!

Gosh, I don't remember the days of ticking clocks!

Yes, I do—it brings back
>The old kitchen
>Where mother put a boy's painting
>Of the old Brimfield house
>And the clock pinged each hour with
>A ding, ding, ding, ding, ding, ding!

When I went to my first pastorate
>I moved into a beautiful modern
>house on the hillside.

It was winterized with a kitchen range
>And a one-pipe furnace,

With water by gravity flow from a spring further up the hillside,
>And clocks.

Kitchen clock, grandfather's clock, mantle clock, alarm clock,
Wall clock, and more—

All before the day of the unnoticed hum of electric timekeepers.

Ties to Time and Myself

I would wind all the clocks and that first night I woke up
    Every hour by the hour!

BONG!   BONG!   BONG!

    Bing Bing Bing Bing Bing

La Sol Ti Do—Ti Do Sol La!!

Tick-tock, tick-tock—You do get used to it and not hear

But the rhythm is there, keeping you going—

Memories—

Who, Me?

One of most thoughtful occupations
Is picking my toes.
I rub and rub
And meditate on the day.
Pleasurable sweat
And a rest
From bickering.
I get myself
Ready to relax
After running
And pushing my conscience
And being afraid to take a nap
For fear I would be thought lazy.
I resolve a few things before bed.
Like—Who's worried?
Feet of warm flesh
Like other people.

0-595-32453-3

Printed in the United States
20784LVS00008B/7-15